MENTAL CONDITIONING

Life's G.P.S.

ELLIOT ALLEN

Elliot Allen
Queens, New York

Limits of Liability ~ Disclaimer
The author and publisher shall not be liable for your misuse of this material. This book is strictly for informational and educational purposes. The author and publisher do not guarantee that anyone following these techniques, suggestions, tips, ideas, or strategies will become successful. The author and publisher shall have neither liability nor responsibility to anyone concerning any loss or damage caused, or alleged to be caused, directly or indirectly by the information contained in this book.

Cover Design: Panagiotis Lampridis
Editing-Interior Layout: The Self-Publishing Maven
Formatting: Panagiotis Lampridis

ISBN: 978-0-9994307-0-5

Printed in the United States of America

Acknowledgements

The process and never ending journey of Mental Conditioning for me began on September 16, 1967, the day my parents were married. While my life did not start until seven years later (September 1974), the 'Foundation' for my Mental Conditioning began in 1967. So with great praise and honor, I give life-long thanks to my parents Mary and Charles Allen for planting the seeds of strong Mental Conditioning which have prepared me for an unbelievable range of experiences that have built my mental strength and continues to do so daily. Those seeds have allowed me to bloom into a man who is willing to keep building a foundation of mental strength to navigate through life and get to my all-inclusive destinations.

However, like every living thing on the Earth I need nourishment to grow. I am truly fortunate and grateful to say I have found my nourishment in my beautiful wife, Michele. She is the water that keeps me in full bloom. I want to acknowledge her as a critical component in keeping my foundation strong.

My wife's nourishment has helped in the process of adding new branches and big branches in our life named Isiah and Aaron. Our boys provide an excellent 'Big Picture' for us to pass on the process of building the strong foundation of Mental Conditioning. The process is never ending, and the support of these special people is truly the power source in my life's navigational system. Thank you, Team Allen!

Dedication

To every individual's Mental Strength and the Mental Conditioning Movement. On this journey, it has been said that I must find a target audience. Yes at times I am obviously speaking to specific audiences, but the beauty of us as a people is that we're all different, but have the common feature of possessing a mind.

We all have goals and 'Big Pictures' in life, and the reward of getting there can be described as our all-inclusive 5-star resort where instead of being a short vacation, can be a permanent way of living. Through Mental Conditioning let's begin the process of putting in our reservations!

I dedicate this book to all of our minds and the Mental Conditioning Movement that will greatly aid every one of us to get to our all-inclusive destinations in life.

Introduction

Our minds are the navigation system that directs of our lives. Each one of us possesses the mental power to take us to our life's goals. The only limitation to our mental strength is what we allow, and the reality is, the process of growing our mental strength is firmly in our hands. Many people enjoy watching a great movie or television show. The suspense and sometimes agony of waiting to see the outcome is unbearable. At times the result is hugely disappointing, and we wish we could change it. Unfortunately, in real life, this is not possible because we have no control over the script.

Our lives are filled with challenges, happiness, obstacles, sadness, turns, and twists, as well as a whole lifetime of different scenarios. However, in contrast to a movie or television show, we can write our scripts. Imagine that, the ability to write the scripts to our lives. Yes, we do that every day whether we realize it or not.

The recognition of writing your own life's script automatically brings responsibility. That strong sense of responsibility manifests itself into feelings of ownership.

Let's look at this, just by retraining and conditioning

our minds it puts us in a position to write the script for our lives and OWN it. Ownership is probably one of the most potent words that exist in society. Let's use the example of being a musical artist who may have the greatest ability on the planet to write and produce music. He or she can write thousands of songs in which no other writer or producer can come close to their quality. With correlation to our Mental Conditioning and training, that individual must first believe that they possess the ability to be the best writer/producer on the planet. Their belief starts the process of writing a life's script. Now, this individual may also possess one of the most dynamic singing voices on the planet. Once you put that singing voice together with writing/producing skills and making some of the finest music, the world has ever seen. Is that not contributing heavily to writing the script of your life? It is inevitable!

The next part of that in which Mental Conditioning will guide us is equally compelling. The artist can write/produce and sing the most powerful songs that reach tremendous success on the radio, the internet, and overall sales. However, if that artist does not copyright his/her song and own his/her masters, they will have a script for their life but no OWNERSHIP. With no ownership, you then allow others to come in and change YOUR script of YOUR Life.

I challenge and implore you reader to fully understand that the conditioning of our minds is the actual key to writing the script of our lives and owning it.

This book will provide the formula to build mental strength. The exercises discussed in each chapter are quite challenging, but for maximum results, I suggest you read a chapter and give yourself a day or two to mentally digest before moving on to the next. However, implementing what you learn into your mental diet is the key to building your Mental Conditioning. Make no mistake; Mental Conditioning is a marathon, not a sprint.

To run a marathon, you have to train your body to endure the long term. We will be experiencing the same intense training while reading this book. Instead of being in a real gym, we will be working out in our mental gyms. One of the most practical resources we use during our physical training in the gym is a personal trainer. That personal trainer is a guide for us to set in motion a plan of workouts to strengthen our body. Equally as important, that trainer is there to always remind us of the plan, the overall techniques, and the goals. Anyone who has ever worked with or seen a personal trainer in action can understand their level of annoyance at times. The level of redundancy can be sickening at times, but this is an essential part of training. So I ask you, the reader, to use this book as your personal Mental Conditioning trainer. Be advised the work in the gym will be challenging. Yes at times the instructions will be redundant. It is important to remember that all of this is for a purpose. With that said, the first exercise is already upon us.

Question: "What do I want for myself?" I believe a common answer for most of us is just to get better! The reply may seem trivial, but by admitting that to ourselves, we have performed our first exercise. The proceeding exercises will be challenging, but constant reminders from your personal Mental Conditioning trainer (this book) are in place to keep you moving and growing Mental Strength. Always remember the Mental Gym is always open and membership is FREE!

Contents

Chapter 1

Mental Conditioning – Self-Evaluation

Before we can begin to build our Mental Conditioning, we must first give it a definition!! Understanding exactly what conditioning is essential to building any part of our body. When an individual physically conditions their body, certain exercises are used to build certain muscles in the body. The beauty of physical conditioning is that there is a visual result. We can look in a mirror and physically see the effects of the exercises we are performing on our body. The visual reward is the most gratifying thing to watch for that individual taking part. The sight of a bulging bicep or a flatter tummy shows that tangible result which motivates them to keep going and push harder for even better physical conditioning and visual results.

Now when we look at Mental Conditioning, the first notable difference is there is obviously no physical or visual result that you can see with just looking in a mirror. Then, so what is it? *Mental Conditioning is the strengthening of our minds to enhance our decision-making skills toward our big picture while staying the course.* Many layers go into our decision-making, which is, the absolute cornerstone of our existence as human beings. We make hundreds of decisions within the first hours of waking up from a night's sleep. Decision making is 100% responsible for our life's direction, and the beauty is, it's totally up to us as individuals. As we condition our minds, we enhance our decision making, ultimately strengthening our life's direction.

The process of Mental Conditioning our minds just as physically conditioning our bodies is a difficult, tedious, process to maintain on a constant, and one, that many give up on, and don't ever attempt to try. Just as in physical conditioning, Mental Conditioning requires many different strengthening exercises to build various parts of the mind. Each exercise exhausts your mind to the point of pain. However, the result increases the ability to maximize your decision-making skills. Now that we have a definition of what it is, we can now break down the categories of strengthening and how each of them affects us.

The order in which we start the process of increasing our Mental Conditioning is truly an individual choice; however, there is a beginning step that must be addressed first with no deviations. The first step is Self-Evaluation!!

This first step is by far the most challenging, and it requires lots of honesty. It is essential that one be brutally honest with self because honesty is the backbone of the whole process. Failure to be frank at this first stage will keep the entire process from starting. There are benefits to being honest with ourselves during self-evaluation for this action will open the gate to all the endless possibilities we see in our future. Honesty is also essential to maximizing our potential in personal and professional relationships, career goals, vision, the pursuit of goals and vision, and just our overall direction in life. This step cannot be devalued.

As individuals, it is a daunting task to look at ourselves and admit flaws, inept qualities, and deficiencies.

Consequently, this is one of the most useful and powerful exercises to the process of building mental strength and opens the door to expand your mental capabilities. There is a saying, "There can be no success without setbacks!" With that thought in mind, how can we expect success if we cannot identify our setbacks? During our journey of having successes and setbacks, many adjustments will be made. This is an illustration of how this exercise can clear the pathway to proceed further in the Self-Evaluation stage.

One key thing to remember about self-evaluation is that every individual is, of course, different therefore the steps each one uses for evaluation are unique. There is no wrong method for self-evaluation, only a bad result. And that possesses a lack of honesty during the assessment.

What do we need to look at during self-evaluation? There are a variety of areas within our basic characteristics to evaluate. These unique traits dictate the manner in which we navigate through the critical phases of our lives. They dictate our decision-making process.

Two Self-Evaluation questions you can use as a base are:

"What are my strengths?"

"What are my weaknesses?"

For some individuals identifying their strengths will be a straightforward process. The opposite is that some people will have difficulties identifying what they do well. The challenge of this test is to train your mind to identify situations you are dealing with. Our decision-making process is based on the exposure of what we have in a given situation. On job interviews, many times two self-evaluation test questions come up. In actuality, the interviewer is not necessarily looking for that interviewee to come up with particularly impressive "strengths" or non-impactful "weaknesses." They are looking for an individual who can identify what they have. Once the identification is made, it's a sign of a person putting themselves in a position to be a real decision maker.

Now when applying this test question to our lives the principle is just the same however the actual answers are now much more important. Those strengths and weaknesses we identify will greatly aid us in the navigation of our everyday life journey and help keep us on the course.

A critical component of forcing yourself to be honest during self-evaluation is understanding the REWARD. You may ask, what is the REWARD?

As we go through the process of self-evaluation, we begin gaining noticeable and increased confidence in who we are. That confidence is coming from identifying and accepting who we are as individuals. Positive and negative traits command equal space in the makeup of our personalities. We can effectively use both to enhance the decision-making process of our lives. Now comes the best part—ADJUSTMENT. One of the benefits of increased Mental Conditioning is the ability to make adjustments! The individuals with the strongest MENTAL CONDITIONING make the best ADJUSTMENTS. Remember the key ingredient to our success or failures in our lives is our decision-making skills. Even the most prudent decisions don't end up with the desired result we were looking to have. Now is when the adjustment phase comes into play. When it comes to changes, we must be very aware that it's predicated on strong self-evaluation.

When describing the self-evaluation stage, it is truly the foundation of the whole Mental Conditioning process. As we state the definition again: *The strengthening our mind to enhance our decision-making skills toward our big picture while staying the course*. In matching up with our definition, the self-evaluation stage is "the strengthening of our minds." It is the process of getting our minds prepared for being able to handle the rigorous training we will endure to gain mental strength. Here is another example.

Many people start off the New Year making resolutions to lose weight and get in better physical shape. While commendable and a good thing to do for overall healthiness, it's contrary to what we may try to trick our minds to believe. The topic of healthiness is not a miracle process with automatic success just because it's the day after December 31st of the given year. The reality is that we must prepare our bodies for the process. We cannot expect or believe that as of January 1st without any prior preparation that we will be able to step into a gym and do 5 miles on a treadmill at a rapid running pace. Furthermore, be able to perform a multitude of exercises for an hour and a half. The truth is it's just not possible without preparing our bodies first. We have to gradually work our bodies to be able to perform these things. We have to change our diet and eating habits to give our bodies the energy needed to sustain the physical challenges we are asking of it. What happens when we don't prepare our body for this conditioning? The whole process of physical conditioning will never get started. Subsequently, the process of disappointment does. The truth is that it is an unwarranted disappointment because we never put in the preparation to successfully initiate the process.

Before we leave self-evaluation, there is one last exercise we must utilize. That exercise is TRUST!! After you have gone through all the painstaking questions and analysis of yourself and evaluated your strengths and weaknesses, the answers you come up with must be TRUSTED. We can continue the parallel of physical conditioning to illustrate the point. When an individual is in the gym putting in hard work lifting weights, at some point, they trust the work put in has made them strong enough to add heavier weights to their routine. If there is no trust, there is no progress or "reward." You have to believe that the foundation will never let your decision making down. That foundation of mental strength is what gives us the ability to make adjustments. When you're able to that, you are now ready to further build your Mental Conditioning by incorporating those answers into your goals and aspirations.

Chapter 2

Mental Conditioning – Adjustments

Earlier we talked a little bit about adjustments and how they play a significant role in building our mental muscle. Let's take a closer look at how making adjustments affect our mental strength. It can become a bit tricky because previously we highlighted the importance of trusting our foundation. Be mindful that trust must hold firm throughout all stages of building our mental muscle. However, will there be times in which our self-evaluations will have to be adjusted? The answer is a resounding yes! If an individual has to at some point go back and fix parts of their self-evaluation should that cause them to lose trust in their initial evaluation exercises? The answer is no! Sometimes the circumstances of life will force you to make unforeseen adjustments. For example, an individual who evaluated his/herself as being someone who easily excels socially may become uncomfortable attending certain events that actually may be relevant towards their goals. For starters, this would not necessarily be a reason to question their initial evaluation, but an example of a life circumstance causing an individual to adjust. The first action would be to take a look at the things that caused this change in their initial evaluation. Possibly intimidation can be a factor. Maybe intimidation of an individual or particular situation is causing a shift from the usual strong characteristics.

Trust is still the dominant course of action, but an adjustment must be made. The individual must still TRUST that they have outstanding social skills, but recognize that an adjustment is needed to show that skill set. In this particular case maybe bringing along another individual as a deflector or point of ease will put them back into their comfort zone. Once there, they can now get back to being the social butterfly they used to be.

In this particular example, we see two MENTAL MUSCLE Exercises working at the same time. We have our all-important foundation of self-evaluation. If self-evaluation breaks down, it is possible that this person would give up and decide not to go to the social gathering. It is severely damaging when an individual feels their self-evaluated strong points become a source of inferiority. However, by making this adjustment, they can identify the origin of that inferiority feeling and bring back the comfortability.

So in recap, when faced with situations that cause challenges to one's self-evaluated characteristics, the first course of action is to identify the challenge. Once identified, adjust! Trusting your self-evaluation and using adjustments with the confidence to overcome challenging situations dramatically increases your mental strength in ways that will be visible to you.

I used the previous example because it was an adjustment I had to make. For me, my identified characteristic was that of very shy, socially uncomfortable person. All throughout my years of elementary school, all the way through college, and into my working career I suffered from severe social anxiety. I still suffer from this anxiety today. There came the point in my life in which through a business venture I was requested to sit in on a few self-empowerment seminars. I hesitantly agreed, but I convinced myself that it was for my business venture which had nothing to do with speaking at the time. When I attended the workshops, something happened within me that I had to evaluate. As I listened during the interactive workshop, I found myself very stimulated by the conversation. I knew I had something powerfully compelling to add. Gradually the adjustment was taking place, and I was able to speak up more during the workshops. I started to get a real sense of satisfaction to talk to people in groups and share what I was learning. How could this be? ME?? Was I wrong about my self-evaluation of not being comfortable socially? No, I wasn't wrong, BUT it had me to learn one of the most profound lessons to building superior mental muscle! Until this day, I still have high anxiety attending social events of any kind. Yes, I do have anxiety when I have to speak. So my self-evaluation is correct. However, I learned that because I found a calling in wanting to share my message, I was able to make the adjustments mentally of allowing myself to work around an IDENTIFIED character trait that would have otherwise stopped me. Again, adjustments of this magnitude are very challenging because it can raise questions about your self-evaluation (your foundation). However, it is strengthening your foundation.

We have now established our foundation of building our mental muscle and understand the basic exercises that must continuously be used throughout the never-ending journey of Mental Conditioning. Let's further the process of testing those mental muscles that are beginning to grow. As earlier stated, *Mental Conditioning is the strengthening of our mind to enhance our decision-making skills toward our big picture while staying the course*. Let's go a little deeper and show how we turn that into the advancement of our lives.

In life, we all have goals, aspirations, visions, and overall standards of life we want to achieve. Profoundly the whole process of achievement is based on decision making. So we see right here, our Mental Conditioning at the highest possible levels enhances our outlook on those goals, aspirations, visions, and overall standards of living.

As we start to look closely at the decision-making process, we will again see the importance of the self-evaluation foundation built. Staying the course is also something that we will see how important of a role our mental muscle plays in nurturing that.

At this point, it's like the excitement of physical conditioning about your body and starting to see those biceps grow in size and definition. It gives you a new found motivation and determination to go to the gym, eat the right foods, and have discipline. Our Mental Conditioning process should be the same at this point. The excitement should be building as you start to see your decision making become more profound. One key compartment we must remember is to enjoy and embrace the process.

Chapter 3

Our Big Picture

Now we can start to look at how building our mental muscle allows increased opportunities in our life's journey. You may ask how mental conditioning affects our big picture. Our Big Picture is without a doubt the most intimate, personal thoughts we can have. When we raise our Mental Conditioning to a high level, we acquire the uncanny ability to stay focused on our goal not allowing any challenge, obstacle, or anything otherwise to disrupt our ultimate objective.

Let's take a quick detour and define what exactly a Big Picture is. As we break it down, we will look at how our mental muscle brings our Big Picture to the forefront no matter how heavy the weight of the tasks ahead. So what are the ingredients for creating the formula for your Big Picture?

- Your Big Picture must be clear and concise
- Your Big Picture must be unique to what YOU see
- Your Big Picture is NEVER wrong
- Your Big Picture can be modified, but only by YOU

- Your Big Picture must be YOURS

- Plan your Big Picture through its entire journey

Step 1: Clear and Concise

Having Mental Muscle is essential as you conceive your clear and concise Big Picture.

We take for granted the difficulty of having a clear thought. The everyday challenges of life often cloud our judgment on numerous decisions made daily. When in the process of formulating the Big Picture the magnitude of distractions become much greater. Remember one of the biggest payoffs to building superior mental muscle is the ability to stay sharply focused on the BIG PICTURE and staying the course during this process. Your mind must be free of distractions. As my pen is writing these words right now, I am on the course of exercising my clear and concise moment. To get to this point, I had to overcome the obstacle that could've certainly clouded my vision, which was, I've never written a book before, and I don't know anyone personally that has ever written one.

My passion drives my hard work and dedication to build Mental Conditioning. Writing about what it can do for anyone who believes in it is a significant part of my Big Picture. However, is that something people will share my passion for doing? Will I be able to deliver the message? The questions could and would undoubtedly cloud my vision if I allowed it. However, as I continually build my mental strength, it becomes much more identifiable that these questions are distractions which take away from my ability to make the clear and concise decisions for my goal.

Now is when you get a chance to build on that foundation we talked about in beginning stages. Now we're at the equivalent of being able to look in that mirror and physically start to see the mental muscles begin to expand and ripple. You start to gain the mental confidence and feel you can easily weed out the distractions and formulate that Big Picture.

Step 2: Unique to What You See

When going through this process, one must remember the all-important foundation exercise of self-evaluation. Let's look again how the process of Mental Conditioning directly affects this stage of our Big Picture. A good example is the fingerprints on our hands. They're unique to every individual. However, unlike our fingerprints, our Big Picture can be altered by outside influences. One can formulate a unique Big Picture, but due to many factors, the vision can get modified outside of the guidelines set by the said individual. The formulation stage should be an exciting time as you mentally develop different ideas to realize your Big Picture. The anticipation of moving forward and putting your vision in motion becomes palpable, and at some point, will take form for others to see. The uniqueness of your goal will be tested heavily in this part. As humans, we have an instinctive reaction to reject things new or unfamiliar. The fact is your Big Picture will be just that to the rest of the world with a possible result of rejecting your "Idea" by those you present it to. There will be enormous pressure to modify YOUR Big Picture to a point where it is more familiar and comfortable to others. Often, many of us fall into this trap, and this is the point where our mental muscle has to come through and lift the weight of uncertainty brought on by others rejection. Our Mental Condition allows us to see the end and stay the course. Furthermore, in this test, the uniqueness of our vision will be challenged, but our mental muscle will allow us to fight the temptation to conform to what others think.

Conformity would be short term gratification and narrows the picture and the direction of our lives. Modifying your vision to conform to others opinion takes you off the course you set for yourself thus leading you in the direction of uncertainty. In life, we all have individuals who inspire us and set a standard in which we would like to follow and surpass. Reader, I challenge you to reflect on the mental decisions you've had to make in the past.

Mr. Walt Disney personally and greatly inspires me. Yes, the founder of Walt Disney World. I believe he is one of the great visionaries the world has ever seen. While I am a huge fan of the Walt Disney Parks, it's not what directly inspires me. Mr. Disney had a vision never seen. An idea that required him to make moves everyone close to him probably classified as insane. He bought over 27,000 acres of swamp land (SWAMP LAND!!) in Florida with the vision of creating Walt Disney World. Yes, it does take business savvy to navigate the deals of buying all this land, but the most impressive and inspiring part of this was his mental strength.

Our Big Picture is the unique idea formulated in each individuals thinking. Most times our Big Picture has very bold concepts and with quite impressive ideas. However as impressive, unique, bold, and creative as our visions are the real key essential ingredient is our mental muscle. Unfortunately, if your Big Picture dies, it will significantly stunt your ability to grow your mental muscle to the next level which is Execution. As we go through these different phases of building, you will see how these pieces fit together like a puzzle. As stated earlier there is no real order to put pieces together (aside from the self-evaluation stage) they will fit regardless. Typically at this phase of conditioning after the Big Picture is formed your mental muscles are ready to begin Execution exercises!

Step 3: NEVER Wrong

Your Big Picture is never wrong. And is truly the excitement of building Mental Muscle. In going through the steps leading to formulating your Big Picture, you have assured yourself "OWNERSHIP." I believe that every one of us has unique characteristics which result in different ideas to form your Big Picture. It is outside influences that take away an individual's confidence to stand by and present his/her ideas. Take a look at some things in our society that have become essential, but think about how the idea was possibly perceived when introduced.

I have always been fascinated by products like Post-It Notes; a simple product of a little note paper with adhesive on the back of it. Did you know that the adhesive was an accidental discovery? Later the idea was born to attach it to the back of a small note size paper.

An idea initially rejected for many years by the company 3M for various reasons with the main one being the lack of possible public interest. However through the persistence of a gentleman named Spencer Silver Post-Its is an essential part of our everyday lives.

Not listening to others beliefs that something is wrong is a challenge to our mental state. Taking ownership of our Big Picture puts us in a right frame of mind to push past others opinion. The key exercise of "trusting" your self-evaluation is very relevant. The result is gaining the confidence that you are never wrong in your Big Picture.

Step 4: Modified by You Only

We just establish our Big Picture when properly formulated can never be wrong. There will, however, be occasions in which our Big Picture will need to be modified. That is okay as long as the modification comes strictly from the individual who owns the Big Picture. Formulating our Big Picture is an exhilarating time in our lives. It is the beginning of a great mental accomplishment. It is a natural instinct to want to share and begin the process of putting your Big Picture in motion. At this point, some of the greatest challenges to our mental strength lie ahead. As you present your Big Picture to others, it will possibly be subject to modification by others. We naturally may think that the "others" is referring to our enemies and those that don't want to see us succeed. That may be, but it may be the ones closest to us. We have to remember that we can only make any modifications. Our natural instinct as human beings to please others will become a challenge here. We must bear in mind, the mental exercises we used to get to this point. Trusting your self-evaluation with our enhanced decision-making skills would be the recommended mental activity in this case.

Step 5: Must be YOURS

Taking a step back, we must remember the Big Picture formulated must be ours. There are many reasons why the formulation of the Big Picture may not be yours. We all go through struggles of life and want the best situations for ourselves. At times hearing another person's Big Picture is very attractive. It can sound like the direction you would like to go in your life. Adopting someone else's big picture is a recipe for failure. We have talked at length about using our self-evaluation as a foundation for formulating our Big Picture, essential because the pieces will match together on the journey. Whatever skills or tools needed traveling toward your Big Picture will only be providing to those owning the vision. Always remember we can imitate, but can't duplicate.

Step 6: Plan the entire journey

There is great significance in being able to plan your Big Picture through its entire journey. The apparent significance is the basic concept of planning. The legendary college basketball coach John Wooden once stated, "Failing to Plan is Planning to Fail." This step provided checks and balances for previous Big Picture steps. To plan anything through, you must have a clear and concise vision:

Step 1. The idea must be unique to what you see to stay on a path through the detours that will come up.

Step 2. You must have the confidence that the vision is correct in what you want.

Step 3. Although we are planning the vision for its entire journey, mentally we must plan for modifications and adjustments.

Step 4. If the vision is not ours, there is no way we can plan through its entirety. The frustration of trying to plan a Big Picture that is not your own will have devastating effects on your mental muscle. On the other side, the process of planning YOUR Big Picture through its entire journey gives a great sense of confidence and reinforces your sense of "OWNERSHIP."

As we look at these six steps, we will need further exercises to help us stay disciplined. In the next chapter, we look at two specific exercises to strengthen the commitment to our steps of formulating our Big Picture.

Chapter 4

Execution and Commitment

What does execution mean to our Mental Conditioning? How does the exercise of execution build our strength? Let's take a closer look at this mental exercise called Execution.

Here I will provide another illustration to show why the self-evaluation stage is the first and mandatory exercise in building our Mental Conditioning. The things we learn about ourselves in self-evaluation stage will entirely dictate the course of action we will follow in maximizing our execution. Let's back up for a second and define execution.

When we look at what execution means to our lives, it is our desire to make our Big Picture a reality and the steps we're willing to take toward achievement. Execution demonstrates the commitment we make to our lives to get to where we want to be. A whole new set of questions will be asked as you execute and commit to the process necessary to achieve your goals. Now how does this tie into the all-important mental strengthening of our minds? Again this is where we start to put more pieces of the puzzle together!

Your honest execution of self-evaluation will pay BIG dividends. The Mental Conditioning Process is starting to take form, and now we begin to see the beauty of, first, self-evaluation, and now execution. As we go through the journey in life toward our Big Picture whether it's personal (i.e., marriage, relationships, desired lifestyles) or professional (i.e., career, financial goals), the path is quite littered with obstacles which I like to call Fatty Foods to our brain. These foods ultimately break down our mental muscle. In the instance of physically conditioning our bodies, we learn what foods we must eat to maximize and keep our body muscle strong. So how do we do this in conditioning our minds? You will now see why correctly and honestly assessing who we are is critical.

Most visions die during the execution phase because individuals are not willing to commit to the necessary steps to execute the desired goal. An example would be starting a business. We hear people say "I want my own business!" The truth is a lot of times the business is a formative idea that can certainly be successful. However, always remember the majority of the times it's not the idea that fails, it's the execution. The execution fails due to the lack of desire to follow through. During our self-evaluation stage, we diligently train our minds to match our desires with who we are. Sometimes who we are is not necessarily in line with what we want. We may want to have our own business, but the reality is we must match up our work ethic to the level of responsibility and the overall Big Picture to be in line with the qualities of being a business owner.

If we do not do this, the commitment and execution will not be there. Fear may overcome the individual. Commitment and fear (equally important as execution), we will carefully examine them later. Keep envisioning the puzzle we are putting together. During self-evaluation if you honestly assess yourself as that individual that wants to own a business and working for someone else is not a viable option then your desire to go through all the necessary steps of execution is natural. If your performance toward becoming a business owner is not there, does that mean wealth is not in the cards? One hundred percent NO! Just the contrary! Matching your desire with who you are, will enable you to rise to the top of the class you're in. Or, as a 9 to 5 worker can you be the best worker a company has ever seen, therefore allowing you to dictate your salary and putting yourself into a position to live a wealthy lifestyle? One hundred percent YES! The key component is understanding and accepting who you are. This ladies and gentlemen are finely conditioned MENTAL MUSCLES!

Please understand this level of execution is not easy to reach. Mental Conditioning itself is something that one has to have the desire to do which will lead to the implementation of the previously stated and future steps. Just as in physical conditioning, everyone knows by performing reps with weights will build impressive looking muscles. Without matching the desire to who you are, one cannot go through the execution of picking up those weights when tired and muscles are aching, and there are options for activity more inviting. Here we see how the mental strength is dominant over physical strength! WOW!! If your mind is not willing to go through with the execution of going to the mental gym and picking up those weights, it doesn't matter how physically strong you may be or look, maintaining the execution isn't possible.

As we go through these different exercises to build our Mental Conditioning, there are tests to help us gauge our progress. I challenge you, reader, to keep strict focus knowing that mental strength is truly the driving force behind everything that we do in our lives. Reflecting on previous life experiences is the tool I encourage everyone to use as we progress in improving our mental strength. Look back at past crossroad situations in your life and ask the question—how would things have been different if I had a better understanding of using my Mental Conditioning to execute what I was doing at that time? How would a more accurate self-evaluation process have affected a particular situation? These challenges will show you how pertinent self-evaluation and execution are to our mental strength.

As we finish with our Execution exercises, it will lead us into the next mental activity of Commitment.

Commitment and Execution go hand in hand. As we go along this journey of building our mental strength, we will see how these practices are married to work in unison to maximize our mental conditioning. At the same time sticking to the persistent goal which allows self to see the Big Picture when making decisions.

So how specifically does commitment play a role in our mental gym? Another exercise in which failure to commit can destroy all previous work done. Our commitment is the source of staying on course and driving toward the Big Picture. There are many pitfalls in which our commitment can be waivered. One persistent pitfall as mentioned in one of the six steps to formulating our Big Picture is the questioning of our decision making by others. Remember, they're not at fault because it's impossible for them to see what only you can.

However, this is now where we have to learn to rely on our commitment when individuals question our decision making. Their opinion can be the beginning stage of us defaulting on our commitment to our vision. The ripple effect is us no longer making decisions or moving toward the goal; compromising the very decisions, values, and basic foundation building exercises that were the backbone of the vision. Or even worse, due to the frustration of others not understanding your decision, you lose the sense of commitment. Once you lose commitment, you lose the path to the goal and ultimately your Big Picture. The second fold is the battle within yourself while enduring the circumstances of the journey. Every decision you will make may not go as planned. Again, adjustments are made along the way. Adjust often! Wavering commitment...NEVER!

So how does this correlate to our commitment and our Mental Conditioning? When defining commitment, please understand that it's another checks and balances to keep you on track toward your goals, visions, and ultimately your Big Picture. After doing our self-evaluations, we start to take hard stances on our commitments. We make decisions based on our commitments. Now, this is where we have to pay attention to the exercise of commitment in our Mental Conditioning. Some decisions will stray from what was initially thought. It is with a strong emphasis that I warn you to be careful. DO NOT allow some decision-making shortcomings to diminish your commitment. Many individuals fall into this trap. Again, this is where you must go back to the first and most important exercise of SELF-EVALUATION. Remember, Self-Evaluation is the foundation of the whole Mental Conditioning process, and the proceeding activities are just rooms built within you. When buying a house, one of the most important steps is the inspection. A critical test during inspection is the test performed on the foundation of the house. Rooms are essential, but it must be clear, they can be easily repaired, and modified and additional rooms can be added at will or even eliminated if necessary. However, if the foundation isn't laid correctly, you can't add rooms or do anything. The process is flawed and will eventually crack and fall. So the lesson here is to believe in your foundation because it will give you the confidence and ability to repair, modify, or take away rooms.

A real life example is Dr. Martin Luther King, Jr. As I sit here and write about his commitment, it sends chills up my spine. Here is an example of an individual who selflessly committed his life to what he believed. In his last speech, Dr. King talks about his vision of getting to the Promised Land. However, he eerily predicts he will not get there with us. For a man to predict his fate of death is the ultimate commitment. If he had seen his future, could he have compromised his commitment and made decisions to try to preserve his life? I certainly believe that could have been the case if he chose to. However, I believe his self-evaluation and his commitment allowed him to look at his Big Picture and see death by murder and STILL stay committed. Ladies and Gentlemen, there is no more powerful illustration of commitment!

With that said, I am sure the overwhelming majority of us have a Big Picture that does not involve death so there is no reason we can't achieve our goal. We talked earlier about the inability of not physically seeing our mental muscles like our physical muscles. Through our increased execution and commitment a noticeable change will take place in our decision-making skills toward our big picture while staying the course.

This brings up to the point of why people fail to commit. On some occasions, the breakdown in commitment will cause us revisit our original self-evaluation and force us to question our internal honesty. Belaboring the point that honesty about self-evaluation is critical. However, one may take a look back and still feel extremely confident that their self-evaluation was accurate and genuine. Subsequently, they may still be some difficulty with their commitment. Now, this brings us to the probably the single most daunting obstacle to maintaining our Mental Condition and keeping our Big Picture clear------- FEAR!!!

Chapter 4.5

Quick Review As We Move On

Before we begin looking at Fear, let's briefly recap what we have examined in the process of building our Mental Conditioning. We defined it as *the strengthening our mind to enhance our decision-making skills toward our big picture while staying the course.* Next, we discussed the steps. The first step which we spent a lot of time on was <u>Self-Evaluation</u>. Through Self-Evaluation our <u>Big Picture</u> will evolve. We learned that after we form our Big Picture, we must <u>Execute.</u> To maximize our Execution, we learned that <u>Commitment</u> is the key catalyst throughout our Big Picture, Execution, and Commitment.

We have seen that Self-Evaluation is the foundation that makes it all possible. We have looked at the various obstacles that can arise during all of the stages. However, there is one resounding, prevalent, and destructive barrier ever present in every stage of our Mental Conditioning. It's called FEAR! There is no stage of Mental Conditioning immune from the devastating destruction fear can render, including the all-important stage of Self-Evaluation.

Chapter 5

Fear

FEAR is the second most critical stage (ingredient) to building our mental conditioning. There are so many layers to this part of our mental growth.

Fear is unique and polarizing to building our mental muscle, and also, the biggest cause of breaking down our mental muscle we've desperately tried so hard to build. However, it is also a tremendous source of breaking down barriers that will push our mental muscle to epic places unimagined! The push is what makes fear such a polarizing stage. Very much like self-evaluation, it is a very challenging phase of the whole mental conditioning process. No different from all the earlier stages we talked about; fear is predicated on proper self-evaluation. That honest and adequate self-evaluation accurately identifies your real concerns. The only way to deal with our fears is to define them properly. An improper identification of fear is an opportunity to make excuses. Be very careful here. Let's take our time looking at fear and how it can be the minds fatty food to destroy all of the accomplished work, but if used correctly to our advantage, be a supplemental vitamin to boost those mental muscles.

What is Fear? As defined by Google, fear is *"an unpleasant emotion caused by the belief that someone or something is dangerously likely to cause pain or a threat."* Wow! Just by looking at this definition it lays out the challenge we are faced with when dealing with fear. Our emotions frankly are one of the most dominating forces on this earth and the emotion of fear 'can' drive our mental state completely off the road and destroy all we've worked toward accomplishing. As we build the mental muscles, we can control the emotion of fear more and more as our Mental Conditioning becomes fine tuned. The process is sometimes frightening but very exciting! Let's go back and look at self-evaluation stage and go right through all the other Mental Conditioning exercises to see how fear can prominently affect every activity.

Identifying our fears within ourselves just as anything in our self-evaluation is not as simple as one may imagine. For several reasons, an individual would not easily identify an internal fear. One of the most common reasons for difficulty in identifying fear is SHAME. Shame and embarrassment is a key catalyst to most of us not admitting our Fears also, are legitimate emotions that can steer our decision making away from our Big Picture. Everyone is different and will develop their remedies to guard against allowing their feelings to drive them off track. Remember self-evaluation is the most intimate and private relationship you will ever have with self. You can lie to everyone else (not recommending that) but NEVER lie to yourself. The beauty is whatever secrets or admission you make to yourself stay right there with you. Please note and understand sharing these fears with others can subject you to overwhelming shame, embarrassment, and flat out emotional confusion. Those outside influences feed into our fears making them more pronounced when there is no plan in place to control those identified fears. (Remember our chart on formulating the Big Picture)

Take this example into consideration. As children, most were raised with the ideology of growing up, meeting that special person, dating them, and committing to a life of marriage with the kids and a beautiful house with the white picket fence. This line of thinking is especially pressed upon girls as they grow into women. However, it's not for only women; men can feel the same pressures. The truth is that men, as well as women, can experience a genuine fear of commitment. For someone raised with those ideologies having a committed marriage, to now be afraid of commitment would certainly cause lots of shame and embarrassment from within. The shame and embarrassment we believe others will have in us causes us not to identify the fear we have in committing to that relationship. The fear will manifest itself in some ways of which are non-prudent excuses. In this particular example, those excuses will undoubtedly show as blaming everyone else for their failed relationship when the truth is it was sabotaged by the individual.

Let's revisit my own story and relate it to fears and Mental Conditioning.. As I stated earlier in the book, writing a book was never something I aspired to do growing up or in my lifetime. Being able to perform workshops/seminars regarding the principals of Mental Conditioning was totally out of the question of being even a remote possibility. Like many, I suffer from a great fear of speaking in front of people and an even bigger fear of expressing my thoughts and principals to anyone. I can't think of one social setting in which I am comfortable. Ironically the path of my life led me to become familiar with self-empowerment seminars. While I was curious about the concept in which I had no knowledge of, I had absolutely no interest in being a driving force of any kind. However, after attending several of the meetings as a quiet observer, something began to happen.

As I sat there, taking it all in, I began to feel a boiling sensation within to participate more as the weeks went by. Did my fear of speaking in this setting and sharing my principals of Mental Conditioning go way? Not at all! However, my concerns were identified by me during my self-evaluation. Now is where you get a chance to see what I mean a when I talk about enhancing our decision making. As I stated my fears just did not miraculously go away because of this boiling sensation I was experiencing to get involved and share and participate. Allow me to be very clear, that battle that goes on inside your mental gym can rival any sparring session in a world class boxing gym. A lot of us just throw in the towel and quit. Yes, it's very easy to do that and stay safe in your comfort zone. However, the question is, is that really your comfort zone?

For some, the answer is yes. It is a case by case answer. For me, I knew that burning sensation I was feeling was too great to ignore. Yes, I could stay in my comfort zone, adhere to my fear and just continue to sit and listen. However for me, in that particular situation the boiling sensation I was feeling wouldn't allow me to stay in a place of comfort. The pain of the bubbling sensation quickly outweighed the fear of speaking in the group setting and sharing my ideas and principles of Mental Conditioning. It wasn't an easy decision to make and much easier to sit there. However, I realized that the boiling sensation would never go away and made a decision. Remember Mental Conditioning enhances your decision making. Was I willing to endure and live with the boiling sensation for the rest of my life for the benefit of staying in my comfort zone? Be clear; there is no wrong answer, only the answer you have to live with.

I remember something the great Muhammad Ali once said: "There are only two kinds of people in life, those that stand still and those that are willing to take a stand, but when you take a stand you have to be willing to pay the price for it." I knew I couldn't stand still and had to take a stand to share my principles of Mental Conditioning because it could be beneficial to someone. Yes, I also understood there was a price to pay. That price was not to overcome my fears because I know that would never go away. However, I felt I could rely on my mental muscle to control my fears. The questions are, will it work or am I mentally strong enough? The truth is we won't know until we try, but, this is where trusting our mental conditioning we talked about earlier comes on the scene. I can recall deciding to become more vocal in the workshops. With each spoken word and point, I made, I felt a sense of gradual relief. That feeling of relief is becoming greater each opportunity I get to express myself vocally as well as through writing this book. How does this relate to mental strength and dealing with my fears? The overall lesson to be learned in backtracking all of our steps should come into play.

In examining my personal story, let's look at all the steps and how they come together like the pieces to a complicated puzzle to help me deal with my fear through mental strength. Through my self-evaluation, I accurately identified my fear of speaking in a public setting and over-all comfortability socially. At this stage I didn't manage it or resolve it, I just accurately identified it. That identification is my all-important and essential foundation. Through self-evaluation, I formulated a beginning of a Big Picture. Remember my scenario; I had established my fear of social settings. However, faced with a desire to deliver a message to as many people as possible, I saw the effectiveness of the message on a small scale (in the workshops/forum I am attending). The effectiveness of the message inspired me to deliver it to more people and opened my mind to all possible ways to deliver this message of Mental Conditioning. Can you see what was happening? My Big Picture was forming. With that, were my fears automatically released? NO!! However, just within these two steps of Mental Conditioning, we are making significant progress in managing and dealing with our identified fears.

In my case, my desire to work toward my Big Picture allows me the tools to deal with and manage my fears. There is an old saying of "The prize gotta be worth the pain." Now plug in the two steps we just talked about, and you will see the pieces of the puzzle coming together. My "PRIZE" (delivering my message) is worth the "PAIN" (my social anxieties). These two exercises are building mental strength to very high levels and managing my Fears. Let's go even further.

We talked about the importance of Execution stage in building our mental Conditioning. In highlighting my life example, I had to now go through the stage of executing how I can get my message out. That meant planning my own workshops and going out to speak at as many events possible. Does my fear stay right in the forefront of my mind? Indeed, however, that sight of the goal (my prize) allowed me to push through, execute the necessary steps and make best possible decisions to march toward my Big Picture. The journey isn't smooth, and the fear never goes away. However, through mental strength, you're able to navigate in a way unique to you and control those fears. The enhanced decision-making skills will manage your fears that Mental Conditioning gives you. Beware of sharing your concern when you haven't started the execution process. Many others will offer opinions on how you should handle them. Their views may be the way they effectively handled theirs. However, they're not you and vice versa. Respect the uniqueness of you and your decision-making skills to understand and deal with your fears. The work you are putting in at the mental gym won't let you down. Trust in the work and that the pieces of the puzzle are all there.

Next thing we talked about in the process was our commitment. What does fear mean to our mental commitment? Fear plays a huge role and can be a detriment to our commitment without building the mental strength to combat it. Commitment in itself is a naturally challenging thing for us as human beings. The typical results of this challenge are excuses. We start to make excuses to try and explain our lack of commitment. I would challenge those excuses and interject that often time's lack of commitment is caused by fear. When we have fear, what is our natural instinct? RUN! Run as fast as we can!! Commitment can be a very intimidating thing because it seems so final. That feeling of finality causes natural anxiety.

A great illustration of this would be our relationships with others. Sometimes we are for whatever the reason fearful of committing to a relationship. Sometimes previous experiences contribute heavily to this fear. However, this is where we have to trust the Mental Conditioning we're building and not to allow past experiences to define the rest of our lives. Remember we write the script to our lives. Undoubtedly obstacles (experiences) come along to alter the story, but we can write how we will get back on track (STAY THE COURSE). Many individuals have experienced some horrific damaging relationships that have put a caution on all future relationships, which is understandable and natural. However, the people who can train their mind to understand that previous experiences are part of the script but not the ending will be able to reset and commit to a future relationship when the opportunity presents itself. It is always a sad and disappointing thing to see someone have a relationship that has all the ingredients they're looking for but due to lack of commitment caused by previous experiences, fear takes over, and that relationship doesn't move forward. The excuses, we spoke about earlier, begin here within the story. Again we can see how the pieces of the Mental Conditioning puzzle fit together. You can plug this exercise of how fear affects our relationships of all kinds ranging from intimate, professional, parental, family, and life-long friendships.

Before we finish up fears, let's summarize the overall effects it has on our Mental Conditioning. The emotion of fear is tops on the list of affecting our mental strength. The effects, however, are both negative and positive. We just went through in this book some of the early recommended exercises of Mental Condition. We saw how fear has a profound effect on the hard work done to perform mental exercises.

We know that our decision-making skills are a navigational system to our life's direction. Just like our GPS we greatly depend on, if we put an incorrect destination, it will take the wrong final destination. Not because the GPS made a mistake. We put in the false, untrue information. Our decision-making process is not that different. If we lie to ourselves in making a decision, it will take us to places in life we don't desire. Once again, getting off the course!

Fear is a catalyst for not being truthful to ourselves during our decision-making process. At times we can see what the prudent decision would be in a particular situation, but we don't make this decision out of fear of consequences. Hence we find ourselves stuck in the same situations. That lead us "off the course" of our Big Picture. Speaking of our Big Picture finally how does fear play a role in affecting us? Formulating our Big Picture is a Big Part of the process of building our Mental Conditioning. Staying the Course in life is only possible when we have a clear destination. That destination is known as our Big Picture! The beauty of reaching our goal in life is unparalleled. Fear has littered the journey. Right from the beginning, the formulation of the Big Picture is quite a fearful process. We hear things like "Don't dream too big" or "You can't." Always remember we are unique, which means, our destinations and Big Pictures are unique. Our minds are naturally programmed to reject things that are new and unseen. It is scary to go where nobody has ever gone before and more frightening to go there alone. The journey is lonely because only you can visually see your Big Picture. All of these factors lead to tremendous fear of what we see as possible! Many of us allow that fear to block the path hence taking us "off the course." Even more catastrophic is that fear doesn't even allow the Big Picture to form. The wrath and destruction fear can cause in our Mental Conditioning is very significant. However, we must train our minds to turn our fear into fuel to boost us. That fuel drives us to the thing; we want to achieve and gives us the almost surreal mental strength to enhance our decision-making skills toward that Big Picture. The question is what mental exercise can we practice building our mental strength to combat our fears? As earlier and often stated everyone is unique and methods can be different for each.

One of the most effective exercises in managing our fears is recognition. Understand it is very rare that we can just overcome our fears, but they're manageable with Mental Conditioning. Very similar to self-evaluation, honest recognition of our fears is the essential exercise to managing them. That management can later be cashed in as fuel to drive us in our life direction. Here again, we can see the effect of our now bulging mental muscles that will translate into a tremendous amount of courage and confidence in our lives. They will be the seeds planted in our mental state to make adjustments to any situation. As we finish the topic of fear, I want to encourage everyone practice the exercise of embracing your fears and use it to forward your progress.

Chapter 6

The Formula

Over the course of this book, I have provided a guideline workout method for our minds. The possibilities are endless, and the application scenarios we can apply to our lives are unlimited. Before we can begin the process of applying Mental Conditioning, we must execute these 'Foundational' forming exercises in the best possible way. It is very similar to the process of building a brand new house from the ground up, which isn't easy. The most important part of the process is the foundation of the house which must be constructed properly and stable with no shortcuts. There can be many amenities and luxuries built like the finest flooring, windows, doors, and best quality walls. You can have an extravagantly relaxing bathroom, well-equipped kitchen area, the greatest sounding movie theater, as well as an enjoyable game room. In fact, I will even throw in a two-lane bowling alley. However with all of this, if the foundation of the house is built improperly, it's worthless because it will eventually collapse. In fact, all the amenities made to make the house heavier on the foundation will inevitably make it fall.

Our lives have a very similar construction pattern (blueprint). Our Mental Conditioning is our foundation!!

No matter what things we add to our lives, material things, marriage, starting families, careers, etc. These things are not sustainable and prone to collapse without foundation forming mental strength. The process is tedious, difficult, and never ending. However, the information provided is a head start to building the mental muscle needed.

When you have the tools you need, it is now up to us as individuals to get out of the way of the process and let the conditioning of the mind come out. I remember a question I heard asked of the great musical artist/legend Michael Jackson. When asked what he thought was the key ingredient to an artist making great music, his response was for the artist to get out of the way of the music within them and let it come in. He further stated, it is often said that we are our own worst enemy. At times this can be true. However exercising our minds and building that mental strength builds the bond with self! When that bond is strong, it puts us in a position to direct our life wherever we want to go. Allowing the ability to get out the way of our success using your MENTAL CONDITIONING!

Mental Conditioning is truly the driving force behind the direction of our lives, and every aspect of our lives is determined by how we think. The levels of thinking are determined by the work we put into training our minds. There are so many different directions our lives can go.

A final visual exercise I will leave you with is as follows: First, think about an individual you know that is highly successful. That success doesn't necessarily mean monetarily but can involve anything you consider to be extremely successful (i.e., marriage, parenting, lifestyle, etc.). Second, think about an individual you consider being on the opposite end of the spectrum. Think of someone you believe is unsuccessful. Again, this does not necessarily mean monetarily. Now think about those two people and think about what the difference is between them. The only difference is how the two individuals think.

The stated definition for Mental Conditioning acts as a formula to navigate us through life's obstacles successfully. There was a lot of information about strengthening our mind stated throughout this book. The definition aka "The Formula" of Mental Conditioning is something I implore everyone to memorize and utilize on a daily basis. The utilization involves plugging our actual life experiences into the definition. You will see the relevance of the definition to all life's challenges, and it will be a conduit for clearing the path toward our life's destination.

Mental Conditioning is the strengthening of our minds...

To enhance our decision-making skills toward

our big picture while staying the course.